more Fred

Rupert Fawcett likes to think of himself as a cartoonist. His publishers like to think of him as a truly creative artist poised on the precipice of greatness and massive public acclaim. His bank manager wonders when he'll get a proper job.

His first book, **Fred,** was enthusiastically received and led to the creation of the popular Fred cards. In **more Fred** we get, well . . . . more Fred.

D0479232

Statics (London) Ltd
41 Standard Road, London NW10 6HF

First published by Statics 1991

Printed in England by H.P.H. Print Ltd.
8 Gorst Road, London NW10 6LE.

ISBN 1-873922-01-9

more Fred

RUPERT FAWCETT

STATICS BOOKS

FRED DIDN'T LIKE BIG
DISPLAYS OF EMOTION

FRED WAS DELIGHTED WITH HIS NEW
SWAMP-EFFECT CARPET

DUE TO SOARING COSTS FRED WAS
FORCED TO CHARGE HIS GUESTS
FOR USE OF THE SOFA

FRED SPENT MANY HOURS RESEARCHING
HIS FORTHCOMING BOOK, 'A DAY IN THE
LIFE OF A TABLE'

PIP LOOKED ALL SET TO WIN THE
DOG-OWNER LOOK-A-LIKE CONTEST

PRIOR TO HIS DENTAL APPOINTMENT
FRED PRACTISED A FEW SCREAMS

FRED LIKED NOTHING MORE THAN A
RELAXING AFTERNOON'S FISHING

FRED GREW ACCUSTOMED TO
PENELOPE'S TANTRUMS

CONSTANCE AND PIP WERE ATTEMPTING
TO BREAK THE RECORD FOR THE
WORLDS LONGEST NON-STOP CUDDLE

FRED FOUND THE NEW COFFEE
TABLE SUSPICIOUSLY QUIET

'LAST WEEK IT WAS MARLON BRANDO, THIS WEEK MICHAEL CAINE,' WHISPERED PENELOPE

PIP HAD DROPPED CRUMBS ON THE
CARPET ONCE TOO OFTEN

IT WAS MRS MUGGINS AND HER
INVISIBLE DOG, DIZZY

FRED COULD ALWAYS DEPEND ON
HIS IN-GROWING TOE NAIL TO
BREAK THE ICE AT PARTIES

FRED'S PRESENT CAME FROM HIS
FAVOURITE GENTLEMAN'S BOUTIQUE

FRED GAVE PIP DIRECTIONS
TO THE BATHROOM

'THERE GOES ANOTHER WEIGHING
SCALES', SIGHED FRED

FRED AND PENELOPE TRIED ON
THE NEW DOUBLE APRON

PENELOPE HAD BECOME CONCERNED
ABOUT FRED SINCE HE LOST THE
KNOBBLY KNEES CONTEST

FRED SEEMED UNCONVINCED ABOUT
THE AUTHENTICITY OF ALFRED'S BEARD

FRED LIKED TO KEEP ABREAST
OF CURRENT AFFAIRS

'LEAVE THE WALNUT WHIP IN
THE AGREED PLACE AND NO
POLICE', THREATENED FRED

AFTER DINNER EVERYONE PLAYED
SPOT-THE-CAT

TUESDAY NIGHT WAS AEROBICS NIGHT

EVERYBODY WAS LOOKING FOR
THE CREAKY FLOORBOARD

FRED AND PENELOPE OPTED FOR A
QUIET EVENING AT HOME WITH
THE CHAINSAWS

FRED WAS HOPELESS UNITED'S
MOST LOYAL SUPPORTER

FRED WAS GOING THROUGH ONE OF
HIS INSECURE PHASES

'WE CALL IT 'TINA TURNER SYNDROME',' SAID THE DOCTOR GRAVELY

FRED WAS EXPERIENCING THE FAMOUS
`BOBBLE-HAT EFFECT`

FRED'S SENSE OF HUMOUR HAD A
CHARACTER ALL OF ITS OWN

FRED'S TEE-SHIRT BUSINESS GOT
OFF TO A PROMISING START

BY THE END OF THE EVENING THE
MEXICAN WAVE WAS ALMOST PERFECT

PENELOPE CERTAINLY KNEW HOW
TO MAKE FRED FEEL SMALL

FRED INVITED HIS GUESTS
INTO THE BATHROOM TO
PLAY HUNT-THE-SOAP

PIP WAS BEGINNING TO WISH
HE'D NEVER MENTIONED
THE MOTH

IT WAS ANOTHER OF FRED'S
PAISLEY ATTACKS

PENELOPE WONDERED IF BUNTY
MIGHT BENEFIT FROM A MORE
SUBTLE APPROACH

'ONE WINE GUM AND HE'S ANYBODY'S,'
GROANED PENELOPE

AS USUAL THE MEN SPENT THE
EVENING TALKING BALLS

'AND WHEN SHE'S HAD HER WAY SHE
JUST ROLLS OVER AND STARTS
SNORING', CONFIDED PIP

FRED WAS ALWAYS PLEASED
TO SEE THE NESBITS

AT TIMES THE TABLE FOOTBALL
COULD GET QUITE DIRTY

FRED COULD ALWAYS TELL WHEN
PENELOPE HAD A SWEET SHERRY
COURSING THROUGH HER VEINS

FRED SPENT THE AFTERNOON
JOB-HUNTING

PEOPLE CAME FROM FAR AND WIDE
FOR A GLIMPSE OF PENELOPE'S
DUST BALLS

IT WAS BIRTHMARKS
AND MOLES NIGHT

'BABY-BOODLE WANTS MUMMY-BUMKIN
TO GIVE HIM A HUGGLE-BUGGLE,'
SAID FRED IGNORING THE GUESTS

'WHY DIDN'T YOU CALL ME SOONER?'
DEMANDED THE CHIN EXPERT

EVERYONE ENCOURAGED FRED'S INTEREST
IN AERIAL PHOTOGRAPHY

BETWEEN THE MONTHS OF APRIL AND
SEPTEMBER FRED'S MOUTH WAS
OPEN TO THE PUBLIC

FRED HAD ALWAYS ENJOYED
A SPOT OF D.I.Y.

FRED'S SPOT CREAM REALLY WORKED

FRED SEEMED NOT TO NOTICE
PENELOPE'S I-NEED-A-CUDDLE SIGNALS

FRED HAD NEVER BEEN QUITE THE SAME SINCE
THAT GAME OF CHARADES

FRED KNEW HE COULD ALWAYS TURN TO
HIS FRIENDS IN TIMES OF NEED

'IN A FEW WEEKS YOU'LL LOOK
BACK ON ALL THIS AND LAUGH',
CHIRPED FRED

FRED WAS HORRIFIED TO DISCOVER A RICE CRISPY
IN HIS CORNFLAKE COLLECTION

IT WAS WAY PAST FRED'S BEDTIME